The Al[...] Marie

William Doreski

Many thanks to the editors of the journals in which most of these poems have appeared:

Antioch Review, Architrave, Argestes, Arlington Literary Journal, Art:Mag, Atlanta Review, Babel Tower Notice Board, Brownstone Review, Change Seven, Chattahoochee Review, Cimarron Review, City. River. Tree., Coldnoon, COVID Spring, Dickinson Review, Dodging the Rain, Everyone's American Sweetheart, Greensboro Review, Harvard Review, Home Planet News, 170 Review, Karamu, The Leaflet, Liberty Hill Poetry Review, The Literary Review, Littoral, Lungfish, Mangrove, Mockingbird, Mycelium, Passages North, Otoliths, Poetic Destinations, Poet Lore, Portsmouth Review, Red Eft, Rio Grande Review, River Poets Journal, Salmagundi, Salmon, Seneca Review, Shambles, Slab, Soundings East, Southward, Spittoon, Tofu Ink Arts, Treasure House, Tribe, Twelve Mile Review, Vermont Literary Review, White Pelican Review, Wind, Zone 3.

In memory of Thomas Lux, James Tate, and Bill Knott

Certain critics may feel that such nasty poems ought not to be addressed to anyone—or even written. That is why they are not poets.

—Martin Seymour-Smith on Robert Graves

Contents

The Angel in the Larch

We don't allow gods in our house,
but maybe we should. The angle
of light is correct. The shadows
cast by the larch absorb
excess heat. An angel seated
on a bough regards us with pity.
Yet our tiny house lacks room
for the alpha god most people
hire to stir their soup and souls.
We could hire a dumpster to fill
with heaps of books to make room
for a mermaid sort of creature
that could sleep in the basement
wrapped in a damp sheet. For some,
maybe for us, this is god
or goddess enough to encourage
our kindly if mournful instincts.
But would caring for such a creature
endear us to the universe?
This is the day's great problem,
casting scrap iron in the streets
and inciting wounded people
to argue weak propositions.
The angel in the larch is silent,
offering neither admonition
nor advice. Ask it in for lunch.
This would be a small step toward
a more spiritual experience
we could deposit in our account.

Angels don't take up any space
and they only eat angel food,
of which we have a pantry full.
The morning feels soggy after
a night of rain-colored rain.
The birdsong is tenuous and wan,
the daffodils droop on their stems,
but the angel looks crisply ironed
and a credit to its species.

Flight Plan

A fledgling sparrow trembles
with a nervous effort to fly.
I toss a few crumbs from my scone.

A parent sparrow picks one up,
stuffs it in the fledgling's beak.
With a chirp of enlightenment,

both birds flutter and soar away.
The hot day has served itself
sizzling on asphalt. Humans pushing

strollers bare themselves, hardly
decent, sweat oiling their hides
as they order iced mocha lattes

at the friendly walk-up window.
Their toddlers slump like sacks
of grain, drooling as they doze.

No wonder Stevens noted
tinsel in August, no wonder
his speaker caught an ice crystal

amid the fidgets of summer flame.
The ice in all those beige lattes
might congeal into a fist

and smite the unwary when
the imagination relaxes
in a modest drone of crickets.

That fledgling had to think itself
into flight, but not over-think
so that its senses lose their grip.

No wind today. A moment
for novice aviators like me
at sixteen, piloting a small plane

over a maze of tobacco fields.
No one fed me a magic crumb,
but my instructor ate a sandwich,

and with a full-mouth mumble
advised me to watch the horizon,
and this time try not to crash.

Like Ovid

People expect me to understand how Ovid felt when exiled to the Black Sea. I would enjoy a lonely stretch of coast where egrets and cranes nest and hunt for tiny fish they can swallow without chewing. Like Ovid I would spend most of my time writing, risking the emperor's further disapproval. Augustus was a prude, and hated Ovid's *Amors*. I don't know what he thought of the *Metamorphoses*, but I would take them, rather than the love poems, as my model. I would write about people metamorphosing not into trees or fish or birds or rocks but machines. Not robots— those nineteen-fifties science fiction wheezes. But massive construction equipment: power shovels, tall dump trucks, bulldozers, derricks, hundred-thousand-watt generators. Personified, these machines would form a diesel-fueled society that my little poems would explore the way a mole explores Hades. No emperors have survived to criticize my work or enforce my exile. No one cares what I write except for the shore birds and the crew of a passing oil tanker headed for the Bosporus. They wave, and the one literate fellow among them says (in Russian), "That guy looks like Ovid. I wonder if we could get him to recite some dirty poems."

Best Practice

Athletic complex parking lot.
The sky's too tall to shield us
from rambling viral infections

so we've parked in orderly rows
for orderly inoculation.
The National Guard directs

the parking and drinks the coffee.
The Styrofoam cups boil over
as entropy reclaims energy.

We sulk and feign great patience
and wonder if the shots will hurt
enough to convince us they work.

A soldier in camo fatigues
and padded winterproof vest
asks questions shaped like sickles.

We answer with our usual blunt force
and he smirks away, satisfied.
Such exchanges behind masks

clarify this cloudy moment.
We've grown to enjoy such banter—
grim purpose honed to incise.

A clutch of nurses confers.
Some sport trays of bottled vaccine
while other cuddle tablets

stoked with private information
that seeps into the frozen light
with gray imperceptible whispers.

At last the injection approaches.
In T-shirt I'm an easy target,
but you must roll up your sweater.

Two sudden punctures, then done.
Emergency flashers on
to indicate we've been baptized

into a modern mode of faith.
For fifteen minutes we await
sudden and fatal reaction.

Slightly disappointed, we drive off
down an ice-dappled road, leaving
something inoffensive behind.

Creation Myth

After months of rain the valley
fills with drab runoff and drowns.
My father and I drive north
toward the hills, but the highway
dips into an endless lake
so we have to park beside a clutch
of houses still on high ground.

The first one's abandoned. We loot
the fridge for beer and cheese and sit
in deck chairs overlooking the flood.
But we aren't the last people left.
From another house a woman
steps, waves to us. Her bathing suit
glistens like silk. Her long gray hair

dangles in dripping locks. Her daughter,
nineteen or so, stands beside her.
We're all marooned here together,
the woman says, let's enjoy it.
The power's still on. A sailboat
flickers in a cove. Only at night,
though, when distant lamplight twinkles,

are we convinced we're not alone.
On the second day the daughter
informs me that under the code
of castaways we're married,
and shrugs off her bathing suit

and entwines me in fantasies
for which I've always been too old.

Her mother enjoins my father
in gestures of equal pertinence.
He seems thirty years younger;
his hair's growing back, thick
and dark and muscular. We regret
nothing, but the rain continues,
the lake rising an inch every day.

Eventually we'll build a raft
and drift till we find higher ground,
or until we prove the planet
isn't round after all, but flat
as a pie plate and brimming
with flood, the perfect surface
on which to sin and sin forever.

.Steeplebush

In the month of steeplebush
a few years after Frost's death
I'm browsing his Ripton cabin.

A sibilance flows through it,
rustling the yellowed pages
of Modern Library books

arranged like country gravestones.
When I lie on his musty daybed
with its blue cotton coverlet

I see myself white and wrinkled
in landscapes smutty with flowers.
Steeplebush flaunts among them,

along with Joe-Pye weed, tansy,
yarrow, Queen Anne's lace. At the foot
of Temple Mountain, fifty years

after my one trip to Ripton,
I slog along in my aches and pains,
still determined to hike myself

into a glory of fitness
unattainable in my eighth
decade. The fresh August sun

hones shadows as brisk as blades.
I still remember the feel
of Frost's mournful possessions—

sharpened pencils left on the desk,
an armchair sagging from use,
a shabby green sweater on a hook.

No one will bother preserving
the hole I leave in the atmosphere.
But maybe on this modest slope

my presence might invoke the pink
of steeplebush, as if the light
were giving birth to itself.

Stained-Glass Colors

Bright winter Sundays, stained-glass
colors draped over the pews.
I ushered elderly couples,
seating them so gently their dentures
stayed firmly clamped while they sang
tremendous mouthfuls of hymn.

Then home to a roast the color
of fine old English leather.
Pinned to cork bulletin boards,
those Sundays linger in glazed
sermons delivered according
to the latest, greatest theologies.

After sixty years of ennui,
I huddle alone as deities
murmur over the airwaves—
their frequency so high only dogs
can make out every command.
No stained-glass colors puddling

on the floor of my garage where
I crouch before a wood stove
to absorb and savor the heat.
These dull snow-tinted Sundays
prepare me for the absolute dark
my childhood denied could happen.

The spirits on the radio boast
of creations yet to animate.
The listening dogs bark and howl
in praise or terror while I make out
only a word or two of Greek.
The wood stove crackles and smiles.

I could write a hundred sermons
for myself, all true and glistening
with lard, but no one else
would believe them, the lack of stained-
glass colors indicting me
and the voices I'd learned to trust.

Holy Water

Only the Devil drinks it
to excess. Priests baptize with it
and sprinkle the altar to purge
the traces of disbelief
that otherwise would eventually
encrust it like barnacles.
In our wayward youth Roy and I

stole and drank an entire font
to incite the visions we thought
must follow. Instead of knights guarding
the Grail atop a foggy mountain
we saw men in black robes bending
young boys over communion rails
and sodomizing them so harshly

several died on the spot, their blood
thick as roofing cement. The priests,
if that's who they were, glared at us,
so we ran and hid in the barn
behind old Mrs. La Roux's house.
In the dusty litter in the loft
we crouched in terror and heard voices

snarl in a foreign language
I'm sure was New Testament Greek.
We heard the black-robed men hunting
for us, tipping barrels and breaking
open boxes. We hardly breathed

until they left. The old saying,
"As the Devil loves holy water,"

meaning he doesn't, never
seemed less true. The devil in us
parched for more, though the priests roving
with their pointed sexual organs
were eager to pierce and drain us
of the visions that otherwise
would surely indict us all.

Like an Old Dutch Landscape Painting

The flaw in the corner of my eye
lurches across my vision
like blood-prints in snow. The path
behind the machine shop hisses
with sleet-fall peppering asphalt.

A compressor groans and hammers
and two men curse each other
trying to unload a big pine crate
from a stake truck. Three kids on bikes
skid along screaming. At the brook,

still unfrozen and flowing like gray
overlapping sheets of metal,
tracks of some hungry creature,
a possum, I think, march across
the pathway and down the bank.

Easy to read the purpose
in that four-footed stride, the trough
where the belly dragged in the grass,
a deeper rut plowed by its nose.
Beyond the bridge a vapor streak

rippled as cellophane rises
from a machine shop vent and curls
into the mist above. I'm shrinking
as I walk, the view expanding
as half the continent unloads

its gloom on New England, expanding
like an old Dutch landscape painting
with human figures perfectly formed
but tiny as the flaw in my eye
and equally hard to focus.

The Old Fort in Agra

Politics has soured our breath
and rendered us ungrammatical.
The light on the snow this morning
looks tainted with colonies
of the most willful bacteria—
those that plunder us organ
by organ until we withdraw
in ashes, grease, and rubble.

You think that peculiar blue
looks less nasty than the bruises
welling around the cat-bites
you receive every night from
our self-tormented Siamese.
You believe that each day offers
the same set of rusty old tools,
although requiring fresh repairs.

But I spot something I glimpsed
at sunrise in Agra, the old fort
steaming with damp and sorrow.
An effect too subtle to photograph
but a brief, distinct undertone
that could trigger unruly mobs
like those swarming the capitol
four days before my birthday.

You don't see how the pieces
of the puzzle fit. They don't:

that's the point. Note the tracks
of an abandoned pet browsing
up to our front door, retreating
with a lingering sigh. One of us
should stay up all night to lure
this lost creature to safety.

You doubt that any life-form
is safe in this stressed climate
with its hundred-year storms
occurring weekly. Yes, the bleached
horizons have warped, but cries
of hunger coiling around us
as we sleep will sour dreams
that otherwise might solve us.

The Railroad Yard In Deerfield

From the dust and cinder driveway
that borders the railroad yard
in Deerfield we watch the freight cars
shrug and jolt and bump in the glare.
Three road units hustle strings
of chemical cars into order,
then unencumbered withdraw
to the diesel service area,

their exhaust throbbing like ego.
What can we learn from the orderly
ladders of glowing rail, the grease-
blackened roadbed, the brown brick
control tower shaped like a tooth?
After an hour of flat cars,
gondolas, and oil-black tank cars
we drive home under cloud cover
heavy as liqueur on the tongue.
Snow tomorrow. But for now

we've an adequate metaphor
of the ordering of knowledge.
Certainly it will disperse,
but in relaxing even slightly
we feel distinctions quicken
into faith, the vivid paint schemes
of a dozen railroads lingering
like praise on the tip of the tongue.
Reading German Aloud

Reading German aloud I let

the gutturals choke in me
like a smoker's cough suppressed
by the pretense of nonchalance:
Wie erg ötzich mich im Kühlen
Dieser schönen Sommernacht!
But here in Fitzwilliam, summer
is still as distant as old age,
the earliest birdsong just breaking
over the gray and icy marsh.
I can't apply the verse of Goethe
to the sonic vacuum of Northern
New England, where languages stall
in the fat full-moon gaze of men
who long to turn their shotguns
on themselves, their wives and children,
and nearest beer-drinking buddies.
The silence is too numb and thick
to notice the weeping of snowmelt
in leathery woods, the scraping
of turtles dragging shells from mud
where they've lain heavily all winter—
a silence so impersonal
St. John of the Cross might mistake
it for virgin humility
and misunderstand the reticence
of the tough old glacial hills.
Reading German aloud I feel
the tongue wrestling with newly
eroticized gyrations that

the landscape won't accommodate,
but to which I can subtly refer
the familiar grunting of men
at the diner, chewing the world
small enough to easily swallow.

Rimbaud, a Self-Elegy

A harsh old photo of Rimbaud
daily stares me down.
Courageous enough to abandon an art
no one can master,
he burns in me like a fear of facts,
an outlaw whose public anger
offended generals and village priests.

Think of Africa,
so eager to devour the adventurer
tired of being shot in the wrists
by disappointed lovers
of indeterminate gender.

Think of the death by cancer,
the sick limb dropped too late,
the smell so rank even nurses cringe
and forget to plump the pillows.

Rimbaud, boy-poet, I'd pray to you
(but never for you)
if I thought you wouldn't laugh,
your brittle cowlick horizontal,
your bow tie crooked,
your gaze already numb as basalt.

The Cupid-bow of your mouth
relents, slightly.
That fooled Verlaine,

but I've learned from my reading.
I won't approach you at all.

Africa calls, the gun trade booming.
But the snowbanks of New England
mirror the absence that filled you
when you were still too young to name it,
your French already too perfect,
your clear eyes acid with shame.

Batik Flannel Dress

Crossing tepid lawns at dusk,
we talk around each other
as if circling some grim monument
of untrimmed, lichened granite.
Your batik flannel dress expresses
the requirements of your body
elegantly as a sentence
by Henry James. Your small talk bristles
with modifiers cut like slate.

Damp smokes from the autumn grass
and smooths your threshing nylon thighs.
I wield my briefcase to prevent
our bodies from brushing each other
and igniting the milky light.
Wooden houses bulk and pass
and the streets crawl under us
and slip away. What have we gained
from all this trembling? The dark

threatens in the east, beyond Beech Hill
where a radio tower winks.
The whole town, illuminated,
ripples with muscled undulation
as if inviting us to relax
with each other, go as limp
as the material of your dress.
If we did that, we'd merge as twins
and begin to live each other

like hermit crabs in alien shells.
The mind is possessive, but soft.
The scent of your body quickens.
Massive shadows rumple the hills
and the streetlamps wink like ideas
in a cartoon world where dimensions
fold and our failure to speak
deeply enough doesn't matter,
the trimmed grass weeping aloud.

The Absence of Marie

The absence of Marie sighs
in hazy urban streets, the lilt
of her alto broken on stone
foundations of vacant tenements

and smothered in rain-damp rooms.
I walk fast to dodge the junkies
and foil the cold weeping south
from Canada. Photos of Marie

posted on brick walls and lampposts
offer rewards. No one but me
knows she's alive but white-haired
and cowering at a table

in the reading room where Sargent
murals dandle overhead.
She's absent in mind and spirit,
her body worn as if turned

on a lathe. That absence sighs
like deflating tires, like politics
sick of second-hand rhetoric.
Marie has begged me to say

nothing, tell no one she survived
a youthful celebrity brief
as the fireworks at the close
of the *1812 Overture*

on the Charles River Esplanade.
Her absence lingers. The posters
assume she's kidnapped, murdered,
or retailed into slavery.

Instead she's researching the fates
of women like her who triumphed
at eighteen, then lost their grip.
She'll waste the rest of her life

in dusty books, brittle manuscripts,
bundles of scented letters. Meanwhile
the reward her family has offered
will go unclaimed. Her absence

will sigh in the windy streets
and people will mistake it
for the lonely collective ghost
of everyone; and the old red brick

of nineteenth-century houses
will blush for her; and my footsteps
will creak in the snow in the streets
like gossip at a funeral.

Kafka in Place

Kafka seated at his desk in the insurance company. He's shuffling important papers, valuable papers, contracts and the dreary reports of actuaries. His salary could support a family, but although he has been engaged to several women, he's too tubercular to marry. He lives in his fiction, his secret undertone. He writes many letters to family and friends, who feel his sour breath lofting over Prague. The days pass like kidney stones. Kafka's stories pile up in little heaps of angst and existential dismay, although the word "existential" would puzzle him. He coughs a lot, but so do most people in this damp gray city. Still, that's good enough reason to call him "Kafka," rather than the more familiar "Franz." He doesn't know that Edmund Wilson will dismiss his work, preferring the graces of Fitzgerald and Hemingway. He doesn't know that his friend Max Brod will preserve his corpse in amber. Those of us who have been to the penal colony and survived that hideous machine, that cosmic bloodletting, appreciate Kafka's attempts to clarify. Those of us who have suffered the knock on the door, the desultory interrogation, who have confessed to whatever doesn't need confessing, accept his blocky little worldview. In memory of his fragile sincerity, we cough up blood and spit it on the sidewalk. Let the post-ward paradigm and all its casual erasures be thus infected, dying at home in bed.

Let's Take a Taxi, Why Not?

We four crowd into a cab.
I'm in the front seat. From Copley
to the museum: one mile.

The cab rockets south, veering
into the urban wilderness.
A short cut, the driver claims,

but the map in my head is tingling.
Neighborhoods of sallow brick
shudder past, encrusted with age.

Streets tangle and knot. Night falls
with a thud that shakes the cab.
Warehouses rear up like Viking

burial mounds. The meter
reads thirty-one dollars. I rip
the key from the ignition

and toss it out the window,
but the cab speeds over a bridge
spanning an oily black river.

Faceless and unlit buildings
threaten with lack of expression.
In the back seat you three agree

we're being kidnapped to Iran
or Somalia. I grab and shake
the driver, who blanches with fear.

The cab rushes on. He whimpers
sorry, sorry, sorry, sorry.
I try to phone for help but

reach only a garble of voices.
The cab crashes into a storefront.
Police arrive. They speak French.

We climb from the wreck, astonished
that this timid cabbie drove us
three thousand miles to Paris

for only thirty-one Euros.
Non, monsieur, a gendarme says.
Not Euros but francs. Plane trees

whisper in vowels more textured
than Boston's. As dawn cranks up
its curtain we tip the tired

and weepy driver and stroll
down Boulevard Saint-Germain
a the day's fresh croissants smile.

Orange County

South of Long Beach the sprawl of light
seems fresh as a field of poppies.
Orange street lamps and orange-lit
concrete office blocks, hotels,
condominiums and shopping malls
engraved on the orange-tainted dark.
Once Costa Mesa grew almonds,
apricots, pears. Now the idling
of big trucks chokes the Southland,
and younger crowds hustle north
along the freeways to sport
on Hollywood, Sunset, and Melrose,
their blue jeans creased like dollar bills.
The empty parking lots assume
the power of the unwritten page.
Security men in blazers
scan their uncharted domain.
I enter my hotel and breathe
the plastic flowers, the spray-mist
panting of desk clerks, the bourbon
oozing from a salesman's pores.
The mind resists, clenched like a slug,
but the elevator prattles up
and I close myself in my room.
At the window, all of Orange County
presses a broad expansive glance
and tries to impose on me
a sense of what's newly possible—
fortunes blazing like natural gas,

autos swarming like piranhas—
and below the surface, the grumble
of tectonic plates describing
the shape of continents to come
long before we're tired of this one.

Raritan

The river strains between highways.
Walking slowly, we feel the weight
drag along beside us, a brine
of grim industrial bleaches
slurred from the dredged mud bottom.

Years of unread books have bowed us.
Our age has begun to show, our hair
as brittle as pasta, our sleep
fitful, still heavy upon us.

The river beside us remembers
thousands of childhoods, but
not ours, and the unfamiliar
sandstone landscape bleeds for
history not our own.

        We can't explain,
but even if we were to walk
underwater for miles and miles
this river wouldn't accept us,
our bones so indigestible
they'd burn in the flow like flint
struck on the dark side of the moon.

Coast Guard Beach

The crosshatched light has suffered
all the way from Spain. Wind rattles
the flags at the Coast Guard station.
A few kites brave the gloom. Your footprints
impress little tide pools. Placing
my feet in them, I feel pebbles
roll like eyeballs in whorls of sand.

A framework spiked from driftwood
huddles against the bluff. Carven
"LOCALS ONLY" warns away
the casual tourist. Charcoal
and a ring of fish-heads and shells
assert that varieties of hunger
distinguish species from species.

Despite the impress of your footprints,
you've never walked this surly beach,
never committed yourself to solving
the presumptions of breaking surf.
Seven hundred miles offshore today,
a tropical storm is rending charts
to detour shipping north and south.
If I followed your footprints
far enough that storm would impale me.

Framed by the driftwood structure,
a shadow precisely like yours
elongates against the grain of light.

I wonder that you'd impose yourself
so boldly on such primal matter.
You gain nothing but worship of stone,
weed and shell—an effort spent
to impress and comfort us both
on some distant parallel plane.

The Wrong Season

Winter enshrines the absence
of negotiable color. Trekking
over the Peterborough Hills
of Thoreau's far-off gaze,
I count my steps to a thousand
and then another thousand.
I picture my abandoned carcass
discovered by hikers next summer,
a tatter of wool and bone.

At home in your homogony
of wood heat and dozing cats
and books you can read in sleep,
you count your steps to ten
and then another ten. Distance
doesn't embrace and cuddle you
the way it does me when thinking
of Li Bai wandering China's
dusty roads and serious rivers.

He never earned a living
despite some favor at court
because he never held his tongue,
even with his life at stake.
I could have been as reckless
if I'd had the steady hand
of the expert calligrapher.
Then even you would admire me
for a moment or two of bliss.

Instead, my clumsy holograph
scrawls behind me in the snow.
Some people might confuse it
with boot-prints. But seeing it
raw on paper they'd realize
that I've tracked myself all over
landscapes and pages equally
illegible, leaving only one
useless but indelible clue.

Winter Purple

Black ice curses asphalt roads
this morning, the moon a white hole
funneling away our dream lives.

Few sharp edges in nature yet
we bleed from tiny scratches
inflicted by our wandering minds.

The challenge of snow-freighted trees
remains critical. One orange spark
of sun won't be bright enough

to disburden the nervous landscape.
December's always the wrong month,
with superstitions running wild

to obviate a year's worth
of whatever we sought to resolve.
Driving to town on black ice

reminds me that learning to dance
pained me like foolish politics.
I prefer my music sitting down,

like you with your love of ballads
going sepia as you listen
to recordings eighty years old.

Driving slowly, all four wheels
on tiptoe, we arrive and park
by the river, where ice floes

crush over the low dam and birds,
mostly juncos and blue jays,
punctuate the colorless sky.

Where have all the purples gone?
Don't you remember how bruised
last winter looked when observed

by the bravest local artists?
We haven't seen them puttering
at their easels for many months.

We haven't smelled their oil paint
or licked our lips over thick
slathers of acrylic: not since

the pandemic arrived, flaunting
its dread symptoms and snuffing
the gist of our public lives.

We still drink coffee outdoors
seated on a cold stone wall
where our friends can see us and wave

from a safe distance. Not even
black ice can keep us at home
all day. But if we skid and crash

we might, in the fatal instant,
recover those purple visions
upon which winter depends.

Watching You Shoot Pool

Watching you shoot pool, the scrawl
of your body re-interpreted,
I'm reminded how cruelly marriage
failed us, how decisively the ghosts
descended from the attics
of ancestral Connecticut homes.

Your latest male friend regards me
with envy as stony as the bed
of a river. What could I tell him?
Beyond the pool hall the village
relaxes in a filmy rain.
All the trees of my childhood

have collapsed or succumbed to chain saws.
Thinking over the terms by which
we parceled our flesh to each other
I agree the bargain afforded
neither mutual nor individual
satisfaction, city apartments

weeping like sealed and icy tombs.
We moved how many times before
the dank odors caught up with us?
You shoot an aggressive but losing
game of pool. No one believes you
when you lower your voice and look

around the room. No one believes you
when I raise my voice and focus

on the target face before me. Bones
grate as your male friend leans over
the table and sinks the nine-ball.
The rain hisses on the metal roof.

I'm going to drive back to New Hampshire
now, leaving you warmly dressed and proud
to have kept your figure all these years.
The highways will unreel in layers
of dark so friable I'll feel
the seams open inside me,

secret hemorrhages to nurture
when I'm a hundred miles away
with my entire life in my hands
and under no obligation
to speak your name or watch your face
flower in dim yellow lamplight.

The Ant-Lion Waits

Your biography has appeared:
a thousand pages of rumor,
psychobabble, flatulence, and cant.

The pages turn like leaves to the rain.
The words are tinsel dangling
from the boughs of balsam fir.

The author mentions me twice,
placing me within half a mile
of your bathing in the Dead Sea

and mooning up at your eyrie
on Central Park South while
you consummated your love for

thousand-dollar a bottle champagne.
Nothing about us eloping
in the shadow of Mount Ararat.

Nothing about our secret children,
who now operate the governments
of three or four small nations

too prosperous to get attention.
As I read this troubled fiction, snow
blurs my vision, September's

favorite freak storm. Crystals
of pure sublime rebuke the book
for its cheaply glued binding

of human skin, its black and white
illustrations so fuzzy no one
will realize they're famous nudes

of Gertrude Stein by Picasso.
You didn't authorize this book,
but coughed up hours of taped

interviews, omitting events
like our fifty years of marriage,
the birth of a dozen heirs,

and our public mutual suicide,
leaving holes into which I tumble
while the eager ant-lion waits

Drinking Tea with Ezra Pound in Venice

Christmas has passed and the light
on the snow has lengthened. Cries
of blue jays toughen like rawhide.
Last night I dreamt that old age

had cornered me, twitched my gizzard,
tripped me into a wheelchair where
I stewed about the good old days
of adolescent passion and wept.

Now the snow-colored sky rehearses
a storm that may not break for hours.
I've time to drive to the landfill,
post office, pharmacy, coffee shop.

I've time to repent all the sins
of maturity, time to commit
fresher and more fervent crimes
to tease the Peterborough police

into issuing press releases
promising to spike the nasty fears
troubling the sleep of children.
I've twenty years before the wheelchair

creaks and the lap robes shroud me
and the books I've left unwritten
flare into swollen itchy boils.
Better not exaggerate. My dream

felt placid and content with itself.
I could've been walking a dog.
I could've been drinking tea
with Ezra Pound in Venice where

stone palazzos have absorbed the cries
of citizens drifting through the close
of centuries. I could've been—
but I was sheepish in a wheelchair

because I'd reached so great an age
my share of the world's resources
had grown so large it shamed me.
Now the snow-light thickens. Carole

still dozes. The cats scratch at the door.
They think they'll be cats forever.
They don't understand how winters
tatter the flesh, how the sky

in stooping so low bares organs
we're not supposed to perceive,
and how deeply in living creatures
such lordly trauma adheres.

Prosaic Enough

A tough-looking crew has flattened the library annex, the newer part where we used to meet for coffee and lectures and political events. Bricks lie scattered in the parking lot, some intact enough to reuse. You want me to gather a wheelbarrow load for your garden, but the crew looks too mean to share. Machinery grinds in the background. A pump sprays a heavy mist to keep the dust down. I guess they removed the books before the bulldozers arrived. I don't see any lying in the rubble. Do you remember those sorry volumes? They were mostly sad old prose, the sort of stuff we speak without knowing that it's prose, or even aware that it's speech. Not a lick of verse except maybe a tattered old Shakespeare no one has browsed in decades. The new library, a couple of years in the future, makes no promises. It may or may not be prosaic enough to communicate with us. It may be bolder and more versified than Shakespeare, or it may be plain-spoken as Harry Truman. It may eschew printed text altogether. I peer through the chain-link fence and admire the determination of the men wrestling their implements. If I were younger, I'd want to join them. Not only to procure your bricks, but to sniff out the last tatters of text. Maybe parsing those clues would render me prosaic enough to please you.

Edible Photographs

Printing edible photographs
is easy. A sheet of lettuce,
pie crust, hamburger patty
shoved into a laser printer.
Push Print, and your photo
emerges in brisk new colors.
You can frame a lettuce photo
and hang it on the wall, saving it
for later. Pie crust and patty
tend to crumble, so eat them
fresh from the printer. What
does this suggest about imagery?
Does some critical theory lurk
behind this palatable art?
We gave up such intellection
when we retired to devote
our lives to cats and casual reading.
Yet the world tosses up pictures
we must preserve for a moment
or two of wry contemplation.
Digital photography renders
the most cluttered scene with clarity
that can sear the optic nerve.
We both prefer film, complete
with tang of toxic chemicals,
the wonders of the darkroom
emerging from red-lit baths.
The grainy black and white prints
of our youth linger like gravestones.

We couldn't imagine treating
such images as confections.
But in this brazen new world
everything's easily digested,
leaving only crumbs and flakes
to represent lifetimes of loss.

Charles and Henry, Henry and Charles

Swinburne wrote of the "light of eyelids," but the hounds of spring were on winter's traces, so of course he got carried away. My friend who collects Swinburne first editions has aged so badly the veils of his soul conceal his expression and render him mute as a stump. No more of this *Atalanta in Calydon* nonsense. Swinburne ended up at The Pines, where he dreamed his masochist dreams of whipping sessions in St. John's Wood. What did all those choruses accomplish? His lean face went askew, the dark arose, and he snuffed. My friend says that's the usual story. But what if those hounds had carried Swinburne off to a well-lit place by the sea, where Henry James, squire of Rye, sunned in his boater? All those heavy lisping novels! Swinburne could have sat beside James in comfortable silence for hours, each thinking in pure but incompatible English. What if my collector friend had joined them, bringing books to autograph? Eventually the sun would hike up its skirts and wade off toward Canada. My friend, of course, being a gentleman, would follow. Then Henry and Charles would share a flask of brandy and congratulate themselves on syntax well spent.

A Bride on the Subway

Sleet whispered on Boston Common
and the skyscrapers dimmed in mist.
Homeless men sat on the stairs
where crowds shuffled underground
to entrain themselves for the suburbs.

I sat across from a couple—
mother and daughter—whose tempers,
expressed in poise and fashion,
engulfed everyone on the train.

Both wore black coats trimmed with mink,
black gloves, patent leather zippered boots,
stylish in a 'Fifties way,
the daughter lovely in profile,
but head-on, tough as a hit-man.

Money, said their alligator bags,
money, money, money. Daughter
clutched a copy of *Bride* magazine,
and she and mother dipped into it,
The crowd of us jarred and jolted
and exited at Harvard,
leaving them cooing and huddled
to plan their gala event.

A bride for the second or even
the third time around, her thin lips
gleaming with brushed pink lacquer.

A bride as white and glacial
as the sleet piling up in the streets;
a bride as poignant as a letter
addressed to a dead man; a bride

so indifferent by the end
of her life her husband, like me,
will believe he's walking forever
under thick urban skies while sleet
embalms him so completely
he won't feel her honed, practiced voice
curdle him like sour cream.

A Meteor

As we drive through the unlit hills a meteor flashes dead ahead,
a silver discharge almost painful in the eye. The earth
with eccentric wanderings has brushed a belt of asteroids,
and gravity has attracted some minor debris that burns
with a bright metallic flame and probably leaves no ash.

That's the scientific ego speaking, that utter faith in fact
none of us question except with the grammar of the unconscious.
But better not bring that up, not with the dark autumn woods
crouched beyond the headlights, each tree a study in form so
complex
I couldn't master it in both our lifetimes. Meteors are simpler
and more like the principle behind the gestures we offer
the world every day. A flash of ignorance and we learn
another tiny fact, another brain cell dead in some good cause.

The silver fire still lingers in the steepest angles of sight,
a glimpse of something so beyond the quotidian we'd like
to frame it, hang it on a wall. What it would then commemorate
would be that movement beyond science when leafless hills
burn without burning, when the eye feels alien worlds swim into
it,
when the footloose spree of matter that constitutes the universe
in a generous impulse gives us a lovely moment of waste.

Norcross Quarry

On the north slope of Ascutney
near the abandoned Norcross Quarry
Indian pipe knuckles up
through the compost of the forest floor
like writing on the palace wall.
We've already been to the top,
our descent thus far as shaky
as Aeneas to the underworld,

our legs as rubbery as the stems
of mushrooms we've seen in abundance.
These woods are unusually ripe,
even for New England. Thirty
or more species of mushroom; acres
of clintonia; balsam as tall
as the quarry-cliff before us.
The view from the top was fluid

and vague with midsummer mist.
The covered bridge at Windsor
stood out like a dueling scar,
but the big Green Mountains failed
to appear, and even Monadnock,
irrepressible but distant,
was too blue to tell from sky.
Now at the quarry we've lowered

our sights, feasting on detail.
Near the scribble of Indian pipe

a long wooden derrick lies
forever exhausted on its side,
eighteen-inch square beams still whole
if deeply weathered, iron fittings
evenly rusted but tough
as when forged, big cables snaking,

still under tension, through the brush.
We could lie down in these ruins
and allow our vegetable hopes
to flourish, as if mourning
all the abandoned industry,
planting our mushroom intellects
on a slope so abrupt we could roll
all the way back to the road.

We could root ourselves more deeply
than landscape usually allows,
but plant life's too isolate
even for us, and the scrawl
of Indian pipe, read too closely,
resembles Dante's Italian,
the perfect language for warning
how bottomless the world is.

Callanish Stone Circle, Isle of Lewis

The avenues and circle form
a rough Celtic cross about
four hundred by a hundred
and forty feet. Standing centered
in the central circle of thirteen

standing stones bathed in sea breeze,
I feel the sky pour over me
in marbled gray sympathies
as if I've finally accepted
the planet's full embrace. The stones,

eight to twelve feet tall, look staid
as the Methodist churchgoers
of my childhood: formal, serious,
but secretly atheist. Traces
of cremation sour the ground

of the cairn underfoot. Science
isn't certain this structure
provided astronomical
or solar function, but the dense
clouds above the Outer Hebrides

suggest that cosmic observations
most often eluded the builders
of this outlook. From inside
the circle I can see the waters
of East Loch Roag and the mountains

of Harris. I think I'll stay here
until history withers away
and the ancient rites refresh themselves
possibly by cremating
whatever remains of me after

five thousand years of patience—
the stones unimpressed, the mountains
plain and stoic, but the waters
of the loch roiling as creatures
step ashore and learn to evolve.

Stone of North Circle, Near the Cove, Avebury

Am I more impressed by the stone,
a notched and corrugated haystack,
or by the neighboring oak embraced
by two dozen ivy vines thicker
than my thigh? The lordly oak
boasts a four-foot diameter trunk
and looks sturdy enough to brace
an Anglo-Saxon Parthenon.

Here everything's suspect, houses
cringing inside the great circle,
overlapped by the central and south
circles, ditched and surrounded
by a white chalk bank. Anything
could happen within this space,
in this timid whitewashed village.

Look at the sheep, grazing fearless
in flat and ordinary pastures.
Note the sheep dog. He's happy
to see me, dashes over for pets
and praise, so proud of himself
for keeping his flock whole and fluffy.

The rotund stone looks dreadful
as some prehistoric monster's skull.
The crease across its middle
suggests a toothless scowl. It's watching

the huge oak tree, waiting for it
to die and fall, the vines tearing loose
and dangling like severed nerves.

The village hunkers down and hopes
the stones aren't as sentient
as they appear. The tree and sheep
don't care, but don't realize
the big stones define this circle
to dominate, not to share.

Decorated Stone, Newgrange Tumulus, County Meath, Ireland

Neolithic, a mass of pebbles
with a few larger stones like this one
inscribed with spirals, diamonds,
herringbone, and scissor-shapes.
I trace the twin spirals, plumbing
the effort to carve them with flints—
the satisfaction of the artist
palpable despite a hundred
centuries of cultural decline.
So much prophesied: the labyrinth
at Knossos, the mazes common
to English country houses, argyle
and tweed, hex signs, magic symbols,
and those creepy eyeless spectacles
that haunted my childhood dreams.
Now that I'm focused I realize
this stone is watching me through
the centrifugal force empowered
by those spirals. I've stared down
eyes painted on Egyptian coffins,
so I'm not intimidated
by this passive if penetrating
stone-age regard. So many
centuries, so little progress
in reading the thoughts of rock.
Carving, sculpture, dynamite
expose nothing but ambitions
so shallow that tracing them,
like sketching Gothic cathedrals,
barely penetrates the flesh.

Former Mythologies

Quesadillas and cold ale from a can. I can't see clearly in the glare of this dim space. The people at the bar might be sparrows on a wire. Big ugly sparrows, mouthing casual obscenities and spewing bar food in gusts of laughter. You look at me with a look I've learned to fear. But not in a supernatural way. I don't buy into the White Goddess nonsense anymore. The only version I ever met in the flesh did indeed eat men like air. But she was nearly illiterate. Her drawn face reflected or refracted the trials of being a single parent. Her husband ran off with the heiress to the treasure of the Sierra Madre. No one has heard from him in several decades. I haven't heard from her since we shared a desperate moment in a field with a view of the Taconics. You never met either goddess or spouse. You can't imagine her sipping ale poured from a can. You've never heard how sinister her kisses, how sinuous her body. You don't want to learn about the years before she moved inland, the long nights in earshot of the sea, the winter surf gnarling onto shore and splaying itself in shivers. You don't want to know how crude she looked in her favorite poses, her teeth sharp enough to drain blood from a stone. Drink your ale and have a slice of quesadilla. Nice and cheesy, the way you like it. Don't skimp on the guacamole. It will taint your breath to ward off white goddesses and the riffraff with whom they associate.

We've Never Been Good Citizens

The hot streets stick to our shoes.
All stem and no foliage,
skyscrapers wilt enough to startle
their inhabitants, who exit
for an early lunch with cocktails.
We've walked enough to earn a seat
outside that tacky sandwich shop
plopped in the middle of the Common
where nothing commercial should be
except the three-card monte sharks.

We've fossilized so gradually
that only paleontologists
note the glaze in our self-regard.
Each summer feels thicker than
the one before. The swan boats,
because of the current pandemic,
haven't left their winter haven,
and ducks keep the pond to themselves.
Crossing Charles Street despite
the ill-wishes of heavy traffic,
we feel smaller for a moment,
as exposed as stones in a field.

We've never been good citizens,
although we often pick up trash
from the sidewalks, always help
blind people across the rush.
We've refused to prosper in shades

of natural vegetation lush enough
to conceal our collections of scars.
We've walked these parallel streets
so hard we've slightly distorted
the city's fragile geography.

The heat sickens and sometimes kills.
The pandemic kills more randomly,
but we aren't afraid of it;
and after a sandwich and beer
we'll walk down to the harbor
for a whiff of sea air ripe enough
to flush contaminants we've hoarded
longer than most people live.

Self-Decapitating

Expert at ignoring pensive
Anglo-Catholic pieties,
I still enjoy a good cry
in a dusty, gloomy cathedral
like Durham, York, or Salisbury.
John Donne's wrought-iron sermons
doctor me into moments
perilously close to belief.
Although I see myself shrouded
like Dean Donne practicing death,
I may never visit England
again, so I'd better dismiss
the soul-wrenching cathedral scenes
and accept the present tense.

You suggest I'm like a sea slug
that self-decapitates to grow
a fresh body free of parasites.
The video you discovered
on the internet intrigues me—
separated head nosing about
its abandoned body, its feelers
serving as surrogate legs.
How does it generate such will?
Yes, shucking my body and growing
a fresh excrescence appeals.
But wouldn't my withered expression
perched atop a new adolescence
look gamey and horrify friends?

Although I prefer to daydream
in my battered leather chair,
maybe I should fly to York.
In the thirteenth century minster
the midnight is deep as the sea.
So many decapitations marred
the reigns of Henry the Eighth
and Queens Mary and Elizabeth
that England must have seemed like
the ocean floor where sea slugs
like me can do without bodies
long enough to grow new ones
purified of competing faiths,
our slime-trails abruptly ended.

Organic Form Revisited

The vegetable slick of a pond
in the woods looks sly as a wound,
a depth burnished with decay.
I could stand till dusk and stare
at the opaque surface and taste

the ambition of protozoa
attempting to combine their cells
the way grammar combines raw phonemes
into cantilevered paragraphs.
Upright pine woods sigh with damp

and glacial boulders hulk and bask.
As a child I'd feared this pond
with its mat of algae and rot.
I'd imagine drowning in it,
terrible hands pulling me under,

dead faces pressed against my own.
Now I know I could wade it
without rolling my pants above
the knee. Why not? I shuck my big
leather boots and wool socks and step

in the muck and let the calm
creep over me. I wade to
the middle, a foot or so deep,
and there the first shy hands
lift from the scum to salute me,

and the dead faces press upward
to make masks of algae that would fit
if I could stoop far enough
to duck cleanly out of my skin,
deflating into the shallows.

A Resurrection

The bird I found apparently dead
in the snow and placed in my pocket
has begun to throb in the heat
indoors. It blinks and its beak
works slowly, biting the air.
I cup the creature in both hands,
pinning wings to body. No need
for a chickadee flying wild
in our four small rooms. No need
for the cats to startle after it,
stampeding down the hallway.
The bird's respiration assumes
a regular nervous rhythm,
so I hustle outdoors and place
the convalescent at the feeder
where it snatches one seed then pumps
its wings and plunges forward and up
into whatever gray life remains
out there. I watch it flutter
into the hemlock forest and hear
perhaps a welcoming chirp.
Then I return indoors to woodstove,
mint tea, and cats too drowsy
to realize how close a prey
had come. The afternoon slopes
to the west, where new storms plot
and make fists against the pink
of dusk. The warmth of the bird
remains tingling in my palms.

I press my hands to my face
and absorb the palpable bird-ness,
the ruff of feathers, the fragile
sense of tiny panicked organs.
If only I could live that close
to flight I'd hardly fear shedding
the flesh to gain momentum.
But when birds are utterly rapt
with metabolic terror
there's nothing to encourage us
also to rise to embrace
the obvious source of light.

Frozen Charlottes

While my partner tends to her ripening clichés, I wander about the shop. A silver-plate tray of Frozen Charlottes. Soaps from Sweden and France. Pillows embroidered with flowers of indeterminate species. Paintings by a local artist I despise for his supercilious little beard. I slump into a cane chair and pretend to doze off. The shopkeeper, alarmed, waves a fifth of expensive small-batch bourbon under my nose. Too early for me, but my partner's so rapt in conversation she won't notice that I'm spoiling my liver. I accept a modest dose and sample it. The varnished flavor ramps over my tongue and retreats to the darkest recess. How elegant, I think, but try to maintain a poker face. The shopkeeper pours herself a healthy shot and we wave our glasses at each other. Another sip, and the Frozen Charlottes stir from their death-pose. If I remain here long enough to earn another dash of spirits, the Charlotte figurines will begin to dance that dance I most fear and admire, the dance that Liszt imagined but never saw performed. The bourbon settles deep in me, where it will do the most good. My partner has harvested most of her clichés and is ready to go. Christmas is upon us, the streets raving with ice and dusted with shoppers toting curious packages. The dead Charlottes sigh so imperceptibly the mist of their lack of breath rises and ghosts out the door, merging with the clammy weather.

Porcupine Treed

With a garden hose I rout
the porcupine under our porch
and drive him up a neighbor's oak,
a bulk of dignity quivering.

From the base of the tree I return
the critter's slow and suffering glance,
thick with terror, its quills jabbed
like Ahab's taunt at the sun.

I would've let it relax
in the cool dark under the porch,
but all six resident cats
showed too much curiosity.

Besides, I wanted to see that
big prickly knot of muscle
unlimber, wanted to taste that
musk of fear. The plain June light

quivers with a timid breath.
The cats gather like members
of a séance, and we all look up
into those black eyes looking down.

All those useless quills rattle
as if scripting a protest
in a language that, like Latin,
people respect but can't quite read.

Frog Storm

Frogs drop from dark rainy trees.
Their bodies glow like isotopes.
Driving west from the city, the ill
lit suburbs inclined on a plane,
we expected the hills to welcome us
with the usual stolid grace,
not with this amphibious patter.
By dawn a jelly of frog-gut
will slick the road. Survivors
will have returned to the trees.
We discuss the various frog storms
we've experienced. Yours occurred
on the New York Thruway east
of Utica. Big trucks slithered
and jackknifed in the ooze. Mine
occurred high on the Long Trail
near Camel's Hump. Camped alone,
I let normal rain extinguish
my campfire. Then the frogs fell:
thousands plopping and writhing
on the sloped roof of the shelter.
I felt Egyptian, powerful,
defiant. The frogs hopped through
the ashes of my fire and scattered
the last warm coals. The frogs leaped
in the beam of my flashlight, winked
and withdrew. An hour later
I couldn't find one. Why do frog storms
plague us? Shouldn't we regard them

as the clumsy punctuation
of the autobiographies
we haven't the nerve to write?
Tomorrow we'll hardly recall
the flop of meat on hood and roof,
but the eyes caught in the headlights
will linger like a cruel remark,
and the odor of crushed frog will rise
to indict whole civilizations.

Rheingold

In the dream called "Rheingold" I'm walking
a dusty highway on the plains,
composing a song to induce
a stranger's wife to run away,
not with me but for her own sake,
to allow her bruises to heal.

The sun boils in the startled blue.
No birds sing. The hot smell of grass
sweetens the limp air. The mind
is alone with itself, its crimes
mostly of omission. The dream
requires that I rhyme my final

couplet with "Rheingold"; but slack
as an old man's belly, my meter
refuses to cough up feminine
endings with the thrust of trochees
to prove to the ear they're justified.
The heat's raw and tastes of oil.

Something's dead along the highway,
something terribly human.
I stoop and touch the battered face,
and every feature's familiar.
Nose, eyes, mouth—even a scar
on the left cheekbone, even the chin

with one unlikely dimple
like a crater puckered by lava.
Yet I can't name this cadaver
except to say that I loved him
in a former life, perhaps a dream
that didn't have to rhyme with "Rheingold"—

one in which a half-rhyme might suffice
to close the eyes of the dead and wake
the sleeper to more innocent
varieties of horror: the bold
full moon burning in the window,
the maples corrupt with its fire.

Baudelaire in Keene

After a long walk on tired streets,
through a shopping mall and furniture
warehouse, I prop my depleted flesh
against the bronze railing downtown
beside the waterfall, the same
railing from which Baudelaire,
a hundred and thirty years ago,

hanged himself rather than translate
the third edition of *Leaves of Grass*.
Wearing my twill photographer's vest
with too many zippered pockets,
I'm aware that forcing fiction
to occupy the dimension
of biography is sinful;

yet I do so with furtive glee.
I know that Baudelaire who died
in Paris of more or less natural
causes also swam the Atlantic
to Keene, New Hampshire, and chose
this location for his suicide
because he knew the First Cheshire Bank

would remain financially sound
despite having a famous poet
hang himself from the bronze railing,
and because his rival Walt Whitman
needed a message sent; as when

John Berryman, who leapt the frozen
Mississippi, left a note,

fictitious, to Robert Lowell, reading,
"Your move, Cal." Obviously
the long walk has exhausted me,
so I pinch the pockets of my vest,
locate a candy bar, perch on
the bank steps, lean on the bronze railing
and doze. When I wake I'm Baudelaire

with my black ribbon tie noosed
about me, about the rail,
the river crushing along below;
and those elegant, fatal poems
of which I'm guilty surging
in the cavernous dark I've hidden
behind my tall but rumpled brow.

Res Poetica

Another day slews into the ditch,
jolting its occupants
but suffering only slight damage.
That ship that ran aground
and blocked the Suez Canal,
stifling the China-Europe trade,
has been refloated. Meanwhile
the President has stayed upright
for several uneventful hours
and vaccination against the plague
continues at a moderate rate.
You feed baby food to the cat,
whose digestive system asks
the most awkward questions about
pet food from our local market.
I sit at the computer and fret
over weather and the stock market,
two factors I can't unfold.
The light has hardened like a tusk.
Wind shivers standing timber
and tumbles birds from their nests.
My friends in the suburbs report
a sudden increase in crime
as noon shadows disappear
in the heightening spring glare,
exposing the existentialists.
Downtown where the subway lines
cross in perpetual rumbles
the odor of winter woolens

has already dissipated, leaving
only a whisper of dark nostalgia.
While you box the cat for a trip
to the vet I stare at the screen
and hope the constant turnover
of the calendar doesn't apply
to fixed moments listed above.

My Annual Superannuation

No words linger in my mouth.
The aftertaste is horrible,
but I smile my toothless smile
and pretend to pity the trees
broken by post-historical storms.
But they reject my solicitude—

too busy stabbing at the sky
with their naked and pointed stumps.
You urge me to speak, but crows
pre-empt whatever I think,
and their sudden punctuation
leaves no exclamation unexclaimed.

You insist on driving downtown
in our antique Chevy Impala,
which groans on rubbery springs
and coughs up broken spark plugs
every fifty miles or so.
You park this homely vehicle

the way you'd park a devilish
child at a daycare center.
Yes, I can still think in foolish
but utile metaphors any
high-school teacher would censor
with a slash of blood-red ink.

I'm too old to express the thoughts
of stubby trees and rusty sedans,
too shy to shout birds from the sky,
but I can still claim enough
air space to make my reeking breath
a force to be reckoned with.

Yes, coffee and a plain doughnut
would settle my current unease.
Despite the efforts of thunderstorms
and the quick dim shadows of crows
following wherever I go,
I'm not that difficult to please.

That String-Thing

For many years I've dragged a string
fastened to some part of me
I can't reach or see in a mirror.

Today, though, as I walk to the lake
it tautens, halting me in my tracks.
Sick of the last ideology,

I wield my pocketknife and cut
the string where it doesn't hurt.
I hear a distant clatter of stone

as the colosseum topples in Rome
and the Parthenon in Athens
and Wailing Wall in Jerusalem

and the Great Wall of China.
Graves open in Boston, Salem,
and Brooklyn, releasing the spirits

I've admired and dreaded the most.
In the British Library, Karl Marx
returns with a puzzled expression,

and in Paris, Balzac prowls the streets,
taking copious, incisive notes.
With that long string cut, clothing

unravels on Manhattan streets,
exposing the most exquisite
and post-professional torsos.

Despite the chaos, I reach the lake
and step into the icy water.
with a sigh of sudden content.

As carp try to nibble my toes
the stub-end of the string drops off,
leaving a puckered wound to heal

as slowly and scabbed as it wishes,
allowing me to mistake it
for some loving cosmic kiss.

Einstein's Bicycle

Riding my bike in humid light,
I roll up the landscape behind me,
gouging a bottomless trench.
My bike is ordinary but works
in two dimensions, destroying
time and depth along the way.

Einstein foresaw this bicycle
and claimed that he invented it.
His friends in Princeton laughed,
but then no one has real friends
in Princeton except undergrads
fumbling through sexual adventures.

Einstein predicted that riding
this two-dimensional bicycle
would collect masses of matter
industrial sectors could process
into plastics so inert
they'd survive the hottest nova.

I'm not proud of complying
to this eco-hostile vision,
but am compelled to pump my bike
up the steepest hill, thereby
leveling it. The pain I inflict
on the rural landscape will heal,

but when I enter the city and scrape
the heavy streets into hay rolls,
folding skyscrapers to fit
into breast pockets, stripping art
from museum walls, I'm spoiling
too many favorite geometries.

Exhausted, I park my bike and slump
into a coffee shop while mobs
stampede down to the harbor
to pray to the sea to repeal
the more passionate laws of physics
and grant us a last chance to think.

That Ophelia Look

Like the inhabitants of Cappadocia, I'll carve a house in living rock. We'll be troglodytes, cave dwellers; but of course, we'll have plumbing and electric service. I'll find a large outcrop of soft bedrock: limestone, pumice, tufa, or as in Cappadocia, ignimbrite. Being good with tools, I'll quickly partition a couple of rooms, then run a wire from the nearest power pole and install a few outlets for refrigerator, lights, radio, computer. I think we should use propane for heat, cooking, and hot water. I'll drill a well outside and with an electric pump to fill sink and bathtub and flush the toilet. Septic—I expect to have plenty of space for a good leach field. Have I not convinced you? You're giving me that Ophelia look. You know I hate to feel imperious, overbearing, arrogant, or otherwise princely in your presence. But think about the advantages of a civilized cave dwelling: no rent, modes utility bills, access to natural resources. We'll be troglodytes in style. We'll marinate all winter and come out in spring smelling earthy and bold. The bears do it, but not with hot water and a flush toilet, or a propane range to cook their grubs. What do you say? Don't look as if you'd rather drown yourself. That's been done, and it wasn't pretty.

Ace Tunnel

Drilled through a haunted mountain,
Ace Tunnel sighs a fetid breath.
The railroad abandoned it
and laid fresh track around it
because the murmur of the ghosts
amplified to drown out diesels
and the rock walls glowed with colors
geologists couldn't assay.

Let's walk through it. Moss carpets
the floor, thick pelt muffling footfall,
although voices resound in depth.
Our flashlights seem too feeble
to dent the dark, but the glimmer
of rare minerals incites us
with a sub-sexual fervor
unusual in people our age.

Three-mile trek, groundwater dripping
and the undertone of ghost
a tremor almost too slight to feel.
You aren't afraid of anything
except the slight possibility
of a ghost train running us down.
We stumble on the rotten ties
and splash through stagnant puddles.

The phosphorescence flickers
and tints our faces corpse-pale.

Despite its mildew atmosphere,
the tunnel's innocent enough,
brisk and healthy rats dashing
over our shoes. At the far portal
we gaze out into a landscape,
then turn to retrace our steps.

But we see no glimmer ahead,
where we entered the tunnel,
and blank granite where we stood
in sunlight moments ago.
Ace Tunnel has sealed us inside
itself. The question now is which
of us will first be digested,
and whether one will suffice.

Mirror of Amani-Nataki-Lebte, King of Kush, 6th Century BC

My tarnished face in the silver disk
of this hand mirror overlays
the face of a Sudanese king
dead for twenty-six centuries.

I feel the two-faced sun god,
Amun and Re, sculpted
on the handle, claim me as child
of their bifocal imaginings,

a dream-creature caught in the gloss.
About me the galleries tick
like engines. Voices of school kids
fuel the sensation of movement.

Yet I'm stalled in this mirror
where my face is fractured, corroded.
The deceased king tries to bleed
right through me and expose himself

to the modern world. Does he know
how far the museum in Boston
has taken him from the Sudan?
No more weeping of the Nile,

no more kiss of windy desert.
The corrupt old silver regrets

no image, the sculpted handle
brooks no apostasy. Yet the face

of the king is mostly erased
by my own, and my steel-gray hair,
despite a wiry insistence,
will never pass for a crown.

Visiting My Cousin in Serbia

Christmas crawls over the Balkans
on its knees. Vranje, Niš,
Paraèin. We'd stop for lunch
but fog pouring down the ridges
could be ancestral ghosts, the gargle
of surly rivers may restate
death rattles of recent wars.

Your moustache twitches like bait.
You've never met my cousin
but insisted on guiding me
over these corrugated vistas
scarred by religious excess
we lack the will to understand.
You've never been so excited
in seventy years of postwar gloom.
Yet you admit you've never driven
north of Macedonia before,
never tested the landscapes of
Kosovo, Croatia, Bosnia,
Slovenia.

In the Athens
of your childhood, in Plato's
and Sophocles' Athens, no one
ventured north of Thessaly
because wolves as big as chariots
howled down from cold pine forests
and ripped the hides from travelers

and pulverized their bones with jaws
powerful enough to sever bronze.

Along the side road to Topola,
a metal Quonset hut gleams
with fresh black enamel. "There,"
you claim, "there the dead gather
when the New Year blizzards howl
to discuss the fate of Serbia,
the exaggerated history,
the studied akimbo stance."

We park at a turnout and open
our last bottle of retsina.
A shiver blows over the hills
and the fog feels icy on our hands
and faces. We drink to the dead
of a dozen pointless wars,
then point the car toward the village
where my cousin's country dacha
leers above a quick black stream
wheezing from a scab-shaped mountain,
the gravel road dead-ending
in the grotto of his practiced smile.

Between Belgrade and Zagreb

Between Belgrade and Zagreb the light
slopes like a sheet metal roof.
Diesel trucks on desperate schedules
roar with frustration. Small rivers

froth and fidget through fields gone
coppery with frost. The old Volvo
fights the road, but I clutch the wheel
as if drowning. If you were here

you'd speak a language respected
in the onion-domed churches spiked
in villages groaning with hogs
penned for early winter slaughter.

You'd demand I stop for tea
at a roadside café where men
shaped like pistons would grimace
a hairy brown grimace and shake

my hand to make sure I'm real.
They'd stare so hard at you the teeth
would loosen in their heavy jaws.
I don't know how deeply the wars

of the Nineties plumbed this area,
but no ruins offend the eye—
the forests pouring down the slopes
confident as troupes of dancers

and the streams only slightly tainted
by whispers of blood. You'd laugh
to see how I focus the highway
so firmly in my gaze. The trucks

pass with blue exhaust shuddering,
and a sign warns that Zagreb
lies eighty kilometers ahead.
In that comfortable old city

I'll spot you a dozen times
strolling in your long black coat
but you'll refuse to catch my eye
because relaxed inside your skin

you parade along Fifth Avenue
in the company of men too rich
to find the Balkans on the map—
the gloom of Manhattan blossoming

with Christmas décor that flatters
rather than offend the disbelief
we share the way this landscape
shares a thousand secret wounds.

Cruising the Mediterranean

When friends fall off your yacht
you refuse to rescue them.
The Mediterranean looks dark

this season. The wind from Africa
isn't warm enough to tempt me
to swim, so I toss long lifelines

to snag your friends and drag them
into Palma where we anchor
with a white and sloping view.

Your friends crawl aboard gasping
like sand sharks. I count them:
everyone survived. An official

arrives to sniff our passports
and we indulge him. Mallorca's
wine exceeds the mainland's,

he brags. You tilt your snoot
and he cringes into his boat
and rows sadly back to the pier.

The government won't even grant him
a motor. You laugh and agree
lunch seems appropriate;

so your wilted friends settle
for crumbs of seafood on lettuce
and sips of wine we purchased

while anchored in the old Greek
harbor of Syracuse. Too bad
the ugly storms that still prowl

this sea in search of Jonah
can't catch up with you. So pale
even in your leopard print

bikini, you look almost fragile;
but I know how deeply you browse
even the most brackish sea,

how you bundle yourself in kelp
to sleep so profoundly nothing
can interrupt your fondest dream,

and how you paid for this yacht
by pretending to mistake
your rich husband's blood for wine.

Freud at the Acropolis

Freud at the Acropolis,
1904, his shovel-beard
wagging as he remarks upon
the unreality. I'm there
with my Number Two Kodak
and snap him peering sideways
at the Parthenon, hoping it
won't fade in the Attic glare.

Freud at least believes in the mind,
a blue spark so dynamic
he has savored it by the fistful.
But landscape puzzles him. Why
should a famous place so muddle
perception and memory? I shake
his nervous paw and commend
his *Interpretation of Dreams*.

"Yes, yes, but the marble's so white...."
He peers at me to determine
whether the mental part of me sings
like bronze or dulls like iron.
My camera reassures him.
The blunt lens looks nothing
like an eye, its ignorance
as comforting as a child's.

Freud will become as famous
as the Acropolis, but today

he's a tourist like me, his face
a slab of middle-aged meat,
his German wool suit too heavy
for the static glaze of Athens.
He fondles my camera in awe
of its plainly objective function.

He doesn't know that the click
of the shutter conceals rather than
reveals what it finds, broken marble
no more phallic than the bedrock
from which the ancients cut it.
Only the most evolved gestures,
like sculpture and photography,
indict themselves with such thoughts.

Water Route to Chicago

Your first train trip. The coach rattles
like a can of gravel. Plush seats
reek of spilled food. We quake around
a curve as a view of factories
ripples past, the umber brick so old
it hurts our eyes. The conductor
checks tickets as he swaggers along,
fragrant with forbidden whiskey.

You fear the train, prefer to fly
despite crowds and fake security.
But you've agreed to travel by rail
to Chicago for a conference
on Serbian pop music. Posing
as a couple of sophisticates
for whom the Erie Canal route
is ancient history, we pretend
that cities drab as Syracuse
exist only in the corners
of our expertly corrected eyes.

Actually we're frightened by the rush
of low hills, the highway crossings
gated to protect us, the totter
of the lightweight tubular coaches
snaking through cities so shabby
they belong in one of those nations
we're too old and fragile to visit.
Now the slather of Lake Erie

with its windy surf reminds us
how sullen geography can be.

The conference begins tomorrow.
We'll arrive at dawn in a hush
of air brakes, then taxi five blocks
and enter the conference center
with posture stilted as our faux
Serbian. Underneath our poise,
the hiss of steel wheel on rail
like a pop song's rhythm track
will brace us against the deadweight
of landscape dragging behind us
with the rest of our pointless facts.

Havana

In Havana, square little houses
crawl down to the harbor to die.
In one dark room the writers
suckle great cigars and plot
the novels they're afraid to write,
their beards tingling with pale blue fire.

I want to tell them, "Publish
in New York, where no one reads
even subversive literature," but
my Spanish resembles the cries
of sea gulls adrift on the stink
of tidal flats, and no one cares

anyway, unless the government
publicly indicts the book
and Castro himself burns a copy.
The writers quarrel, their beards
enmeshed; walls creak and telephones
jangle in government offices.

Walking alone through the old city,
I see the streets toss like blankets
on a deathbed, see the shops
pining for lack of goods. Ninety
miles to key West where fishermen
study marlin instead of novels,

where no one has read a book
since Hemingway pelted the walls
of his Idaho house with his brains.
Poor old Havana. Cigar smells
dominate, and traffic's heavy
near the old fort with its view

of the mouth of the harbor. The miles
of open sea breathe stonily
with that patience all conspiracies
require, the island of Cuba
nailed to its collective unconscious
like an untanned pelt to a wall.

Stranded in the Naples Airport

Stranded in the Naples airport,
my ticket and passport stolen,
I feel the cone of Vesuvius
mock me as it mocked Pompeii.
Its symmetry hurts like an insult
in a language half-understood.

The police are indifferent. No use
pursuing so minor a theft
for a foreigner whose lack
of lucrative occupation
has sent him to Europe in clothing
he should've left in a dumpster.

Since I've no money, I walk
from the airport back to the city
on a road lined with concrete blocks
erected since the war blasted half
of Naples flat. Only the bay
remains untouched by the cruelty
I let well up in me, distaste
for a city of bicycle thieves
and shoeshines. Traffic hustles past,
sizzling like gnats. Pastel houses cling
together like giggly little girls.

A thick moustache offers a ride.
He spotted the American's
dirty L. L. Bean jacket

and wants to practice English.
As he drives me to the consul,
we pass a pint of grappa back
and forth between us. Night breaks out
like an unexpected disease.

I ring the consul's bell. No response,
so half-drunk I collapse on the steps
and dream the terrible dream
of losing ticket and passport
at an airport not in Naples
but in Frankfurt, then finding
my corpse tossed into a dumpster
labelled "unfit for research."

When I wake the consul's shaking me,
his face distorted with rage.
Citizens like me, careless and poor,
should revoke themselves. I agree,
but need a new passport anyway,
so I can pretend that all these years
of Freudian dreams and displacements
add up to an identity.

Flight to Iceland

At dawn the corrugations
of glaze on the driveway catch
the morning light and disperse it.
Color now seems important
to calm the dark that quarreled
all night, leaving a salty tang.
Someone's off to Reykjavik
this morning, five hours airtime
with a smack of faded aurora.

From what I know of this person
I doubt that the solar wind
dancing in the Arctic dark
will enhance his stunted persona.
Still, a flight to Iceland offers
an arc of far-flung horizon
sure to expand the space inside
even the thickest old skull-bone.

I've never spoken to this man,
never shaken his massive paw,
but have often seen him guzzling
coffee in the same café where
that famous dissident writer
toppled into his daily latte
and dispersed his keening spirit
in otherwise secret dimensions.

He landed in Iceland the day
he fled the Soviet Union

with backpack of books and papers
and a single change of underwear.
In a worn army shirt issued
in the camp, he looked as limp
as something left out all winter
to atone for being human.

The ice on my driveway wouldn't
impress, depress, or discourage him
after his years in Siberia—
no matter that the dispersion
of sunlight faintly suggests
the Aurora Borealis
with its massive prismatic effects
of green and yellow and violet
to assuage the night within.

A Prose Afternoon

Things dangling from things, rain on snow hissing with melo-drama. How foolish the sun would seem today, peering into desperate places the tides never reach. Once the Antarctic finishes melting the tides will reach everywhere. But for now, we imagine we're inland. Our local fjord doesn't contradict us, and pretends to flow east, always east. The afternoon unrolls its dreary sentences. They all accuse us of aging, aging, aging. Too bad, but the symptoms tell their own story. Even if they lie. Speaking of lies, our dominant politician just flew overhead, screaming his favorite scream. He's on his way to engage his followers, who have summoned him by shouting fractured slogans into the sky. When he lands thirty miles closer to the actual sea he'll gnaw on the crowds, nipping off their little heads and chewing them thoroughly before swallowing. No one minds. He likes hearing the sighs of the Antarctic glaciers soughing off and splashing into the sea. He likes the taste of brain and skull crunched into a gelatinous mass we wouldn't feed to a dog. The rain enshrouds the hemlocks. The snow lies so flat it mistakes itself for a page gone blank with dismay.

Penguin Races

Lining them up is difficult,
since they waddle absently
in several directions at once,
and refuse to face the right way.
Their slick feathers gleam in sloped
cold glare. Their tiny heads
contain a helpless contempt

that with collective exertion
they could focus like a laser.
Finally they're all facing north.
But the bang of the starter pistol
scatters them in four dimensions.
Only one scoots toward the finish,
but he veers to the left to avoid

a random, useless victory.
The long Antarctic summer day
revolves like a wooden waterwheel.
As we sip from our flasks, the penguins
gather to commiserate,
their hard eyes nailed so firmly
in their heads their gaze seems fixed,

but intelligent as X-rays.
Observed from the air, the flocks
form oversized hieroglyphs
that shift in the eye the way speech
does in the ear, momentary
against the blue and green auroras
prancing on the mirrored ice.

Returning to Camp

Returning to camp years later,
I find the wooden barracks
all staring at each other
in mute and mutual witness.
The icy light bares everything:
the pump where we washed at dawn,
the latrines stinking of quicklime,
wooden picnic benches smoothed.

Rampant in that final summer,
as in an old horror movie,
death repealed all decency
and drowned two dismal children,
fumbled one from a treetop,
and bled one with an axe-stroke
aimed at a femoral artery.

After the last, we all went home
because ghosts trilled all night
and blood pooled in nightmares
even the counsellors suffered.
The camp never reopened,
yet despite its lakeside frontage
no one bought the property,
no one even vandalized it.

I'm more alone than anyone
lost on the Antarctic ice sheet.
The barracks groan in the wind,

still repenting. The famous ghosts,
faintly visible in daylight,
sit huddled on a picnic bench.
I call their names, but absorbed
in eternity, they ignore me.

Careful to avoid the blood puddles
left by nightmares sixty years ago,
I cross the yard to the pump,
which despite its patina of rust
still grunts up a gush of water
cold enough to torture boys
lined up naked in the sunrise.
The latrines now smell as sweet
as garden compost in spring.

I want to ask the dead boys
how they get through the winter
in these unheated barracks but
they wouldn't bother to answer
even if they shared my dimension,
which even in life they didn't.

The Princeton Tiger

The train seems reluctant to stop
at Princeton Junction, but does.
The odd smell of New Jersey.
I'd forgotten that dim flavor.
A lengthy walk through Penn's Neck.
The dinky train no longer runs,
its track a slur of rust, the ties
too rotten to bear any weight.

Washington Road seems endless,
the early spring marshes twittering,
Carnegie Lake half-frozen still.
I reach the campus. A ruin,
as they warned me, every building
bulldozed into a rubble heap
spangled with last summer's weeds.
First College, Gauss Hall, McCosh,

the chapel, Firestone Library—
even the trees cut down for lumber
to rebuild the demolished village.
Yet nothing has been rebuilt,
Nassau Street blocked by debris,
one wall of the old hospital
still standing to attest to losses
no one bothered to tabulate.

At the site of the Witherspoon Grill
I recall myself ordering

scrambled eggs and whole wheat toast.
The hiss of the gas grill warmed me
all over. Summer rain splotched
the big windows, my workday
in the library stacks loomed.
Nothing remains of that moment.

Nothing to loot, no souvenirs
to take back to New York where
no one will want to hear how sad
the ruined town and college look.
Five years from now a waste land
of housing development will claim
this site. No one will remember
Nassau Hall and the Battle

of Princeton, no one will recall
the university's buttery stone,
the arrogant undergraduates,
the orange and black tiger motif
that one cruel night opened its jaws
and ingested everything in sight,
leaving only an untold lie
at the corner of Einstein Drive.

Green Fish

With a whiff of borrowed glory,
Amy steps from a burning bush
and flashes me an evil eye.

A rooster crows in the smog.
The sun blinks and withdraws
its tentative April favors.

Some well-meaning volunteer
offers refreshments, wine and cookies.
I don't take such communion,

don't acknowledge the cannibal
instinct directed at deity.
But Amy does, gladly, scooping

a handful of cookies and a plastic
tumbler of the cheapest red.
The singe of flesh clings to her,

but I'm the burn victim weeping
fluids I'll never quite replace.
What has happened here with

social noises abutting us?
Old guilt for old crimes? Crass
and inchoate longings critiqued?

Downslope from this little hall,
formerly a Catholic church,
green fish explore a green brook

sudsing from a cluster of mills
that haven't milled anything
for the last eighty years.

Amy stretches a painted smile
and plasters it to the wall where
it runs like a spatter of blood.

We pretend that this is small talk,
that the green fish are safely
metaphoric, that the church

doesn't retain ghost rituals
subtle enough to ensnare us.
The weak sun whimpers. Maybe

someday we can share a pun;
but not today, the stink of char
brisk all over me, and Amy

brimming with the confidence
of one who fishes for green fish
and always catches her share.

Fin de Siècle

On this rainy August Sunday
the hills creak and toss, and stones
grit in cold swollen brooks. The dream

from which I've risen has left
no sediment, no tiny scars,
no nerve-endings bent like weeds.

Drive downtown, valves hammering, park
at the diner, press my face
to the pages of the *Times*. Faith

can't foster sufficient regard
for the mottled sky to force me
into the Congregational Church

to sing "Onward Christian Soldiers"
or "A Mighty Fortress is Our God";
but merely reciting the titles

emboldens something dark and hairy
to embalm me in its embrace.
When I wake, the whole afternoon

will have flushed downstream, the maples
shivering like beaten foil.
No one will have heard my name cried

aloud by some riptide of clouds.
But the split white glimpse of dusk
will offer its pearls, and the cry

of an unborn child will linger.
Another fin de siècle and I'm caught
pale and naked and unprepared:

this small town wheezing about me,
and the psyche disassembled like
an old car that will never again,

even with expert repairs,
drive the reckless country roads
without sparkplugs pinging with fear.

Alpha Box

Proudly my physician displays
the alpha box assembled for me,
a collection of minerals
that matches, inorganically,
my personal chemistry
and could, in powdered form, someday
rejuvenate me, if scientists
decide how best to administer
so crude a dose. The wooden box
looks like one of Joseph Cornell's.
The minerals are sylvite, a normal
anhydrous halide; jarosite,
a hydrated sulfate; beryl (pink),
a metasilicate; olivine,
an orthosilicate, common;
danburite, a pyrosilicate
in tiny brownish crystals;
microlite and tantalite,
a pair of multiple oxides;
and orpiment, a simple sulfide.
Acmite, augite, and wolframite
complete the collection but
although the last is a tungstate
I'm uncertain if the other two
are meta- or pyro- silicates.
The physician isn't sure,
either, but he swears the collection
perfectly answers my organic
makeup, the composition

I inherited from Adam.
His own alpha box is smaller,
he confides, containing only five
specimens, all of them metallic.
Why am I so complex? The plains
of Eastern Europe lie so flat
because geologically inert,
simple as the bottom of the sea.
No one of my chemical background
should locate his ancestors
in so low and fertile a place.
I peer into my alpha box
and feel the minerals draw me
into their crystalline splendor,
a world ruled by geometry
rather than by peristalsis,
a silence devoid of temper
unlike the house I grew up in.
There my own mineral collection
still crumbles in the basement,
unaware of the resemblance
postulated by scientists
tired of facing a godless
indifferent universe alone.

Amelia's Cube

In her mournful apartment Amelia
has sculpted a rough wooden cube
of planks stolen from building sites.
She invites us to critique it.
Although the apartment's walls
of unrequited flesh already
ripple with warning, we claim

to love the cube for refraining
from the threatening gestures
Amelia's other sculptures
indulge with creaking and moans.
We don't really love it, but fear
to stir up grief in weepy rooms
no one would ever dare enter.

Amelia removes her green wig
and plops it atop her sculpture.
That humanizing touch helps.
We walk around it, cooing
and making kissy faces.
It's too big to fit the doorway
but easy to disassemble,

being screwed together with zinc
decking screws, each plank numbered
like an artifact. It means
something, makes a point the way
bad art always does. Amelia

observes us observing it.
Her face clouds with crystal sparks.

She realizes that we hate it,
hate its hollow bulk and vulgar
joinery, its unpainted planks
embossed with the artist's last will
and testament in characters
only the trees that died for
this clumsy object could read.

Ghost Child

At the foot of the holy mountain
the ghost-woman offers her child.
I fondle the solid form,

flesh-warm. This is not a ghost,
and somehow I'm the father.
But the form dissolves in my hands,

the cry of the infant regresses
in the scream of a magpie,
the ghost-woman breaks up like

an ice floe, and the mountain
stoops to absolve her, the air
tingling where she stood. I weep

myself awake in a rented room
in Pine City, Minnesota.
The air conditioner howls

and the stucco walls press heavily
against me. The distance between
my dream and myself so quickly

expands I've forgotten her touch.
I'd thought the imprint would last
like a fossil, every nuance

sculpted in stone. Light beckons.
The highway groans in a trough.
My ghost-child festers somewhere

in a flash of neurons, a voice
too inarticulate for verbs
or nouns, the unformed brain a slug.

In a whisper of gases the child
drifts over the rumpled plains
a thousand miles to the Rockies,

a mass of complex minerals
generating dreams about ghosts
and an abstract terror of form.

A Thesis Defense

Around the big table by the lake,
a dozen colleagues debate
the future of a graduate
student whose thesis lacks scholarly
intent, the laser-printed pages
corrugated with digressions,
yet flimsy for lack of notes.

The lake slops in a sinkhole,
clumsy and oblique. The cottage,
inherited by a professor,
rears in a woodsy shade of green
popular in my childhood.
From a window the housekeeper peers
at me, her face a meteor

struck from the absolute dark.
My colleagues bristle like houseflies.
As they quarrel over commas
I excuse myself and enter
the cottage where that woman points
upstairs. She's drawn a warm bath.
Together in the drowsy tub

we pull the water over each
other and let the old desires
abate. A brass clock is ticking;
time isn't over. I gasp and rise,
and she embraces me so fully

that we're standing on the bottom
of the lake, where we breathe like fish,

unafraid, all our organs poised
for the next stage of evolution.
The stones begin to speak. They tell me
that long before the glaciers
creased and folded this landscape
I'd pressed my right palm into the mud
and made a fossil print that lies

many layers beneath the lake.
Yes, I remember that handprint,
the tropical vegetation, tracks
of huge but ignorant animals
that dodged me with opaque shadows.
My colleagues gaze at me, expressions
innocent as flour sacks.

Am I ready to vote? I am,
and we accept, twelve to none,
this oddly oblique thesis,
the lake panting and satisfied,
the housekeeper peering still
from an upstairs window, the pines
runic in the tall white sky.

Autumn Infarctions

Along the railroad through the swamp
near Powder Mill Pond the maples
and sumac rattle like shook
metal, each red leaf a wound.

I could walk old railroad embankments
till my heart infarcted and love
fled through the opened manhole,
but then I'd know where the railroads went,

know every splintered tie and rusty
length of rail, understand why aster
and goldenrod fill the gaps
hacked into arbitrary landscape.

No fishermen left, only snarls
of nylon here and there in the trees.
The swamp-water's cold and silken.
As I pass with my camera,

whatever lives there refuses me,
refuses the naked sunlight.
The leaves, stratified in brave pastels,
shimmer like a coat of mail

bloody and glorious with loss.
But something eludes me, the sheen
of open water, the shameless
musculature of the hills. The leaves

slacken as they fall, limp,
raw as bacon, and the swamp water
mirrors me in shades of gray.
The railroad curves out of sight

ahead, cramped by perspective
and formal conventions too basic
for the adult mind to acknowledge
without a quiver of regret.

Writing the Book of Snow

Still writing the Book of Snow,
I slump at my desk as thaw
puddles at my feet and cries
of hungry pets rise and burst.
You brew the witchiest tea
and ply me until my bladder
resurrects the airship *Hindenburg*.

Still the Inuit synonyms
for *drift, icefall, walrus* and *seal*
elude me, pronunciation half
the problem. With due respect
I fondle terms on my lower lip
but feel them slip to the floor
where they mess themselves in melt.

I should stay indoors until
I finish writing this allusive
and moon-slanted book. But you
insist on grocery shopping,
and expect me to steer the cart
while you with breezy instinct
pilfer tired pressboard shelves.

Hear slush lolling from the roof?
Do you want to drive in this muddle?
The Inuit have words for *folly*
but I can't recover them before
you've started the car and shucked me

into my coat and boots and scarf.
We're so tipsy with each other,

the imbalance of our lives pronounced
like the Inuit word for *marriage*.
The slush, sleet, and freezing rain
that shape this pulpy morning
all belong in the Book of Snow,
which I won't get written today.
I should put it off till summer

when flowers wrench the heart and stones
rattle as the brooks dry up in drought.
Then we both will long for winter
and my little book might gather
a few readers primal enough
to try to exhume the written word
from the ignorant grip of the earth

Pants Down for the Apocalypse

Pants down for the Apocalypse!
Apparitions panic the crowd.
In the rush hour on Tremont,
the hammering of sixteen hoofs
trumps the rumble and horn-blow.
Slouched above a urinal
in the Common's shabby men's room,

I'm ready as I'll ever be.
A drunk crumbles on the floor,
dried out of his socks and skin.
Two cops sneer at the wreck,
glad to be out of the storm.
The snowfall's a feint of weather
to suggest the fate of the mob.

I don't think the horsemen can find
me here. "No Animals Allowed"
a notice notes. The attendant groans
in sleep, scratching at his crotch,
dreaming of women or lice.
Should I run? The drunk fades in dust.
The warning bellows again:

Pants down for the Apocalypse!
Now the two cops startle and rush
outdoors to the subway kiosk
and descend. I pose unzipped
as the draft sucks in tatters
of snow, wry proclamations
of trespass scribbled in cold.

Witches' Sabbath

Tadpoles storm out of jelly.
Blackflies and mosquitoes tease us
as we watch the gluten shred,
the essence wrestle into light.
Almost full, the moon sinks wordless

to the bottom of the pool,
its moot, inflected light implicit
with prophecy, its mythic
intentions unfulfilled, its bulk
leaden with self-digestion.

Slowly ripening, a week behind
the frogs' eggs, the pimply transparent
clots of salamander roe
shudder on drowned yellow stalks.
Slick and full-grown salamanders

dangle profiled in the depth,
toes as delicate as dendrites,
tails acute as African thorns.
If only we could swim among them
and share their focus on this pool

we could understand why the moon
has plunged so deeply, why the pool-
reflected moon is rounder
and more substantial than the one
left nailed to the watery sky.

May Day Eve, the Witches' Sabbath,
the dusk woods deepening about us,
the wriggling of tadpoles insistent
as the moment of exclamation
with which our own lives began.

www.ingramcontent.com/pod-product-compliance
Lightning Source LLC
LaVergne TN
LVHW091510170726
843492LV00001B/417